The 10 Commandments of Leadership

Eric Harvey ♦ Steve Ventura

o

WALKTHETALK.COM

WALKTHETALK.COM

Resources for Personal and Professional Success

To order additional copies of this handbook, or for information
about other WALK THE TALK® products and services,
contact us at
1.888.822.9255
or visit
www.walkthetalk.com

THE 10 COMMANDMENTS OF LEADERSHIP

Printed in the United States of America
10 9 8 7 6 5 4 3 2 1

Printed by MultiAd

ISBN 978-1-935537-94-6
51495>

9 781935 537946

CONTENTS

DEDICATION

This book is dedicated to all of the wonderful leaders we have been privileged to work with, and work for, during our professional careers. You have taught us – probably much more than we taught you. You have inspired us. And you have shared your many "secrets" to effective leadership which we've used as the foundational content of this work.

INTRODUCTION

It's an age-old question that has been pondered by millions of people – one that we've spent the better part of our professional careers researching and studying. And it's one of the most important and relevant inquiries you must address as you continue to build and shape your professional career:

What does it take to be a truly effective leader?

A simple enough question – but a fairly *complex* answer!

Why complex? Because of the many variables involved. The myriad of management styles, issues, tasks, technologies, industries, and needs out there in the business world make it challenging to come up with a cookie cutter – "one size fits all" – package of leadership characteristics for everyone in every situation. But while the task is challenging, it's not impossible. And it's one we've set out to tackle within the pages of this work.

Experience Is a Great Teacher

Over the last thirty-plus years, we've had the privilege and good fortune to work with literally thousands of leaders – at all levels – in organizations of all types and sizes. We've taught and consulted ... we've listened and learned. Throughout those experiences, we've observed, analyzed, and documented a collection of core "best in class" leadership beliefs and behaviors. These characteristics – traits which separate *the best* from *the rest* – are what we call ...

THE 10 COMMANDMENTS OF LEADERSHIP

What's in a Name?

Look up the word "commandment" in the dictionary and you will find definitions such as: *an edict; a command or mandate; the act or power of commanding; an order or injunction given by an authority.* Trust us, we're not deluded with thoughts of having some special authority, uncommon wisdom, or right to set rules or mandate behavior. Clearly, those attributes are "way above our pay grades." We both believe in the existence of a higher power – and we both know that neither one of us is it!

So why the label "commandments"? Because of two other dictionary definitions: *precepts; teachings* – which is exactly what this material has been for us ... and what we hope it will be for you. And because the guidelines that follow are IMPORTANT, UNIVERSAL and PROVEN.

They're good. They're right. They work!

Earning Your Title

One of the many things we've learned through our work is that having a leadership position and being a leader are not one and the same. Your position is something you were appointed to ... something you became eligible for by being a good performer in the past. In all likelihood, what you did "yesterday," as an individual contributor, helped you get the title you hold today. And that's exactly what your position is: a classification ... a title. **Being a true leader, however, is significantly different!**

"Leader" is a descriptor – a designation you must *earn* through specific actions and behaviors. It's based on what you do *today*, and what you will do *tomorrow* – not what's printed on your business card or engraved on your name tag. And earning the label of "leader" requires that you think and act in ways that are considerably different from what you did before you were promoted.

Simply put, to be a *real* leader, you must do the things that leaders do ... and you must do them well. Those "things" are THE 10 COMMANDMENTS OF LEADERSHIP.

An Important Role

As a leader, you play a critically important role. People need you. They rely on you. They have expectations of you. And they count on you to know the way, show the way, and LEAD them *along* the way. To be sure, your job is comprised of not-always-equal parts of challenge, frustration, demand, joy, and satisfaction – all topped off with a large helping of responsibility. Being a leader isn't always easy, but it is always important. And when done right, it is – with few exceptions – truly rewarding.

Despite the old adage, leaders are *made* not born. They're made with discipline, commitment, and hard work. Leadership is developed by learning and refining specific skills – and *applying* those skills according to sound principles and time-tested guidelines. Providing you with those guidelines is what this book is all about.

So, pay attention to what you're about to read.

Regardless of whether you're a seasoned manager, a novice just starting in a leadership position, or someone in the middle of the experience continuum, you need to be effective ... you need to be successful. You owe that to your team members and you owe that to your organization. Most importantly, you owe it to YOURSELF.

Read on. Lead on. Choose to be the most effective and respected leader you can be. Follow ...

THE 10 COMMANDMENTS OF LEADERSHIP

Make What Matters Really Matter

A participant in a recent leadership development workshop nailed it when she uttered this gem ...

"Leaders are guardians of importance."

That was her truly profound conclusion to a discussion we conducted based on four simple – but not necessarily easy to answer – questions.

The first question posed to the group – *What's important here?* – produced fairly typical responses which can be summarized with four words: people, performance, principles, and profit.

The second question – *Do those things really matter?* – brought out the predictable (almost robotic) response: "Of course!"

Query number three – *How do you know those things matter?* – required a little more thought but produced equally predictable answers such as: "It's obvious" and "We just know."

Then, came the fourth question – *How do YOUR PEOPLE know what matters?* And this is where the discussion got interesting. A couple of participants rehashed answers from the previous question: "It's obvious" and "They just know." Before we could respond, another member of the group jumped in and challenged those statements. "I'm not so sure our people always *do* know what's important here. If they did, we might not have some of the problems and issues that we periodically deal with. That may be our fault. As leaders, it's up to us to make sure what matters really *does* matter. And I think that's something to do with actions – not with words."

That discussion, that day, was the genesis of this first commandment of leadership.

The Clues

Without question, observing what leaders DO is the true litmus test of what's important for any organization. And employees definitely are watching. They're watching ten specific leadership behaviors that provide clues to what really matters:

1. **What you pay attention to** – the things you look for, notice, and comment on.

2. **What you talk about and emphasize** – the things you discuss in meetings and mention in written communications.

3. **What you do, yourself** – the actions you take, the behaviors you demonstrate, the example you set.

4. **What you expect and demand from others** – the standards you set and requirements you establish for your team.

5. **How you spend your time** – the priorities you establish and activities you engage in daily.

6. **What you budget for and allocate resources to** – the "tools" you provide and activities you fund.

7. **What you measure and evaluate** – the performance and results you monitor, track, and provide feedback on.

8. **What you brag about** – the things you are proud of and cite as examples of positive achievement.

9. **What you reward** – the behaviors, achievements, and results you recognize and reinforce.

10. **What you enforce** – the things you hold people accountable for and assign consequences to.

Fact:
Saying "quality is of utmost importance" is a waste
of breath if the only thing you check, measure,
and reward is the number of units produced!

The Test

Think for a moment about the things that are important in your organi-zation. Jot them down on a piece of paper. Chances are your list includes words and concepts like: our policies and procedures, customer service, quality, profitability, teamwork, responsibility, ethics and integrity, etc.

Next, circle the items on your list that are *really* important … those that *really* matter. (It's okay to circle all of them!)

Finally, review your list, do a little self-reflection, and honestly answer the following:

Would an outsider who was unfamiliar with
our organization know what truly matters
here merely by watching me?

What specific behaviors can I cite as evidence?

Key Strategies

Yes, leaders *are* guardians of importance. YOU are that guardian! You must ensure that what matters to the organization also matters to each member of your team. What can you do to meet that critical leadership responsibility? Here are a few strategies that should help:

■ **Make sure they know.** Don't assume employees inherently grasp what's important in your workplace. Why *would* they? Why *should* they? After all, they view the job through *their* eyes, not yours or senior management's. In order to be sure that team members know what matters, you need to communicate. You have to tell them … you have to discuss it. And that entails meeting with all of your people (individually or as a group) and following this agenda:

    a) Identify the principles, behaviors, and outcomes that matter.
    b) Explain *why* they are important to everyone's success.
    c) Clarify what you expect from all employees.
    d) Confirm team member understanding.

So, meet with your people, complete this agenda, and you'll be able to say with assuredness, "I know they know!"

■ **Keep it in the spotlight.** Things that are important get ongoing attention. They're continually discussed, written about, featured, tracked, measured, and repeated. Let's face it – no employee is going to conclude that something is important because "the boss said something about it last year." The meetings you conduct, the memos and e-mails you send, the coaching sessions you conduct, the training you provide, the behaviors you recognize and reward, the reports you issue, and your postings on walls and bulletin boards (just to name a few) all provide opportunities to reinforce what truly matters. Use them, and remember …

Out of sight, out of mind.
Out of mind, out of importance.
Out of importance, OUT OF PRACTICE!

■ **Hold everyone accountable.** Think about it. What in our adult life, that's truly important, has no associated accountabilities or consequences? The answer is *nothing*. In "the real world," importance and accountability go hand-in-hand. It's important to pay taxes – and we're accountable for doing so. It's important to obey the laws of the land – and we're accountable for doing so. And when it comes to our jobs, there are behavior and performance expectations which are important to meet … and employees MUST be held accountable for doing so! You make that happen by backing up words (stated expectations) with consistent actions (consequences). Albeit distasteful, that is a leadership responsibility that must be faced and met.

Behavior tends to be a product of its consequences.
Without accountabilities – and enforced sanctions for
doing wrong – employees are likely to conclude that
"It doesn't matter what I do!"

■ **INspect what you EXpect.** Stay aware of what's happening in your group by wandering around, observing, and visiting with employees. Keep up with what your people are working on and the behaviors they are exhibiting. Schedule briefings on activities being performed, decisions being made, and results being achieved. Just as certain excuses are unacceptable from team members, here's one that's unacceptable from you as a leader: "I had no idea that was happening."

■ **Model what matters.** As a leader, you have a strong influence on the thoughts and behaviors of your employees – perhaps much stronger than you think. And one of your many leadership responsibilities is to model the behavior you expect from others. To do otherwise is hypocrisy. Fact is, you must *earn* the right to expect things from your people by doing those same things yourself.

Like it or not, you do operate in a fishbowl. Employees are constantly listening to your words and watching your behaviors. They assume that it's okay to do whatever you do; they conclude that the things *you* do are the things that *really* matter. And they are right!

You have no choice about being a role model.
You are one … it comes with the job.
The only choice you have is deciding
which role you will model.

Take Away … to Remember

Importance is not something you assign – it's something you demonstrate through actions and behaviors. To be a truly effective leader for your people and your organization, you need to remember and apply the first commandment of leadership:

MAKE WHAT MATTERS *REALLY* MATTER

PRACTICE
WHAT YOU
PREACH

The second leadership commandment, *Practice what you preach*, is a timeless guiding principle – one that's probably just as familiar to most people as the classic "Golden Rule." It's been passed down from generation to generation, seemingly forever. And while it's one of the most familiar and relevant guidelines for living, it's, far too often, overlooked and seemingly forgotten.

To fully understand the phrase within the context of leadership, we need to examine and define its three component concepts:

Practice, You, and *Preach*

Practice is a pretty clear term. It means *to use, do, apply, show, act, behave,* or *demonstrate*.

You actually has a dual meaning. There's you the individual person and leader, and there is the collective you – the organization's leadership group ("management") of which you are a member (or, at least, *seen* as a member through the eyes of employees). Both meanings apply and are of equal importance.

Preach (or *what is preached*) is the most encompassing term of the three. It's both literal and figurative … spoken and not. And it includes …

Your personal beliefs and values;
Your organization's stated principles and values;
Your organization's policies, procedures, and rules;
What you say is important;
The things for which you hold others accountable.

Simply stated, practicing what you preach means that you DO what you expect from others … that you are "about" what your organization says IT is about.

The Expectations

To paraphrase a timeless biblical lesson, *To whom much is given, much is expected*. And as a leader, much has been given to you. You've been entrusted with authority and discretion ... with increased control of time and resources ... with the care and well-being of the customers you serve. Most importantly, you've been afforded the honor and privilege of leading your organization's most valuable assets – its people.

Your team members know that although they are employed by the organization, they really work for you. So, they look *to* you, and *at* you, for guidance and direction. And just as you have expectations of them, they have expectations of you. They expect you to be trusting and trust-worthy, careful and caring, respectful and respectable, competent and committed. They expect you to abide by the organization's rules and be a steward of its values. And ...

> they expect you to lead by example ...
> to stand for something good and noble ...
> to *walk the talk*.

They *expect* all of that ... and more. They *deserve* all of that ... and more. Meet those expectations and responsibilities, and your success potential is unlimited. Discount or ignore them, and everyone loses.

Everything Counts!

In the game of life, there are no time-outs. Unlike children at play, you don't get to call for do-overs – you don't get to cross your fingers, call a "Mulligan," and claim that something you did doesn't count. Fact is, as an adult, *all* of your actions matter … *everything* you do counts! And that's especially true when it comes to your leadership role.

Think about it. If it's wrong for employees to be irresponsible, then when is it okay for the boss to blame others for his or her mistakes? If it's wrong for team members to lie, then when is it okay for a manager to "fudge" on an expense report or time log? If it's wrong to disrespect others, then when is it okay for the leader to tell derogatory jokes or degrade people "behind their backs"? The answer to all of those questions is the same:

It's never okay!

To believe otherwise is to assume that the importance of doing what's right varies with the circumstances at hand … that those in leadership positions are not bound by the same rules and standards that apply to employees … that team members should do as we say, not as we do. And that's just plain wrong no matter how you cut it.

Facts:
Your actions determine your character.
Your character determines your credibility.
Your credibility determines your ability to lead.

The Ethics Imperative

Doing what's right. Keeping yourself and your people out of trouble. Being a role model for appropriate conduct and business practices. Upholding organizational standards. Earning the respect of others. If those things are as important to you as they should be, then it's critical that you, as a leader, behave ethically and perform with a high level of integrity.

To be sure, "ethics" is a huge and complex subject. But truth be told, the number one (and probably most important) key to always doing what's right is actually quite simple:

THINK BEFORE YOU ACT!

That means checking decisions and planned activities for "rightness" *before* implementing them. Use the questions below (or similar ones supplied by your organization) as your test:

    A. Is it legal?

    B. Does it comply with our rules and guidelines?

    C. Is it in sync with our organizational values?

    D. Will I be comfortable and guilt-free if I do it?

    E. Does it match our stated commitments and guarantees?

    F. Would I do it to my family or friends?

    G. Would I be perfectly okay with someone doing it to me?

    H. Would the most ethical person I know do it?

How to Recognize Leaders Who
Practice What They Preach

Look for people who ...

Keep their promises and honor their commitments.

Really have an "open door."

Follow ALL the rules and regulations.

Treat everyone with courtesy and respect.

Are upbeat and positive.

Tell the truth.

Are polite and considerate.

Are prompt and prepared for work and meetings.

"Own" their behaviors and "own up" to their mistakes.

Think before they act.

Solve problems rather than "celebrate" them.

Pursue win-win outcomes.

Give their best effort.

Display initiative.

Are dedicated to learning and continuous improvement.

Deal with disappointments and setbacks constructively.

Are committed to the organization and its mission.

Are committed to the people they lead.

Do these behaviors and characteristics describe YOU?

The Values Challenge

With few exceptions, all of us – and therefore all of the organizations for which we work – have beliefs, values, standards, and a relatively similar sense of what's right and what's wrong. They are what make us different from other living things on the planet ... they are what make us human.

But while having principles may be natural for us, actually practicing them isn't. Acting according to these beliefs, values, and good intentions is one of the biggest challenges each of us faces every day. We face it as people, we face it as employees, and, unquestionably, we face it as leaders.

To be sure, doing what's right and important – modeling the behavior you expect from others – isn't all that easy. Temptations abound. But that fact provides no rationale or acceptable excuse for behaving otherwise. You have to work at it. You have to stay at it!

Take Away ... to Remember

Guidelines, rules, and principles to live by are just words – unless you actually *live* by them. To be the trusted and respected leader whom others will want to follow, you must abide by the second leadership commandment ... you must:

PRACTICE WHAT YOU PREACH

COMMUNICATE WITH CARE AND CONVICTION

What job-related activity do leaders engage in the most?

COMMUNICATION!

*What job-related activity do leaders typically
pay the least attention to?*

SAME ANSWER!

If you combine all the time you spend making and returning phone calls, sending and responding to emails, writing reports, texting, meeting with coworkers, customers, and vendors, giving instructions, teaching and coaching, making presentations, etc., you will probably find that 70–90% of your total working hours involve some form of communication.

Fact is, you don't just engage in communication – you *rely* on it. It's what you use to inform, instruct, direct, develop, motivate, convince, correct, collaborate, and achieve; it's how you affect performance, build trust, and shape a productive business environment. And since the majority of what you do involves communication, the majority of your success (and your reputation) will be built around how well you do it.

But, communication tends to be the area to which leaders pay the least attention and consequently are often the least skilled. Why? Primarily because most people believe they are better at communicating than they really are. So, they don't think about it … they don't work on it. And they're left perplexed by survey results that continually identify poor communication as "the major problem around here." That's a problem that must be corrected … a problem that YOU must correct. And that's why the third leadership commandment is:

Communicate with Care and Conviction.

Communicating with CARE

Ask most leaders if they "care" about the way they communicate, and you get an immediate no-thought-required response: "Of course!" But follow up by asking what they specifically DO to *demonstrate* that care, and the responses come a lot slower. Much more thought is required to answer that question ... much more thought is required to communicate well.

To be an effective leader, you must be an effective communicator. That means paying careful attention to ...

What you say –the words you use and information you include.
How you say it –your tone, style, and delivery medium.

And then checking ...

What others hear – the messages they receive.
How others react – what they think, feel, and do in response.

It means being considerate of team members' reactions, concerns, and expectations. And it means communicating with others thoughtfully and respectfully.

The best communicators are
CAREFUL and CARING.
The worst are
CAREFREE and CARELESS.

Communicating with CONVICTION

Look up "conviction" in the dictionary and you find a variety of definition sets – two of which are directly applicable to leadership communication:

certainty; confidence; fervor;

and

the act of convincing; the state of being convinced.

Great leaders are passionate and confident – about their jobs, their people, and their organization's mission. And their communications reflect that fact. Read what they write – listen to their words – and you can literally feel their commitment ... you *know* what they stand for. They use terms like "responsibility," "high quality," "service," and "teamwork." They continually emphasize what's important. They tactfully say what they mean. More importantly, they mean what they say. They are direct yet respectful, candid yet considerate, strong but not overbearing.

Great leaders are also great salespeople. They understand that the very best way to get team members "on board" with any goal, project, or initiative involves convincing rather than demanding ... selling rather than telling. So, for them, communication is about more than just building **understanding** – it's also a tool for building **acceptance** and **support**.

How do those leaders build employee acceptance and support? What is it they do? What can YOU do?

   ✓ Use informal, positive, and "user friendly" language.
   ✓ Share your feelings and beliefs – let your passion show.
   ✓ Explain The WHYs as well as The WHATs.
   ✓ Focus on the benefits to be gained by everyone.

Key Strategies

Without question, communication is one of the most important tools in your leadership toolbox. It is a process ... a strategy ... a responsibility ... a key to your overall success. Here are a few strategies to help you maximize the impact and effectiveness of your communication activities:

■ **Start with the end in mind.** Think about what you want to accomplish before you write or speak. Identify your goal – your desired end state. Is your purpose merely to inform? To convince? To inspire? To involve? Complete the sentence: "This communication will be successful if ..." Then, consciously choose words, tone, and message components that logically match your purpose. Effective communication is the product of thinking and planning ... of knowing where you're headed and then mapping out the best route to get there. It's an outcome rather than an activity. Deal with it accordingly!

■ **Focus on quality, not quantity.** Many leaders mistakenly assume that the way to improve communication effectiveness is to just do more of it. But far too often, that makes problems worse rather than better. If the quality of communication is poor to begin with, increasing the amount will only produce more poor communication – and more anger and frustration. You need to provide clear and informative messages that people can understand, accept, and hopefully support. You don't accomplish that by bombarding team members with endless, poorly conceived memos or emails – or through mismanaged meetings that accomplish nothing and waste time in the process. The way you do it is taking the time – and expending the effort – to ensure that each of your communication activities is the best it can be. That's communicating with care.

■ *Listen* **with care.** To communicate with care, you need to be as good at listening as you are at speaking and writing. Effective listening is an active process that requires attention and focus. It's important that you concentrate on the words and behaviors of the speaker – without passing immediate judgment. The key is remembering that the goal of listening is UNDERSTANDING – "I want to hear what you have to say" … "I want to know what you are thinking and feeling" … "I want to learn what the world looks like through your eyes." You don't have to agree with a person's position in order to understand where they're coming from and why they feel as they do. And once you have that knowledge, you'll be better able to work constructively with the employee and establish a relationship built on trust.

Listening is also a demonstration of respect. When you listen to others, you're nonverbally saying: "Your thoughts and ideas are important" … "Your concerns are important" … "YOU are important." The opposite is also true: Failing to listen is a sign of disrespect. That's why you need to recognize and then minimize those behaviors that get in the way of true understanding.

■ **Keep it honest and "real."** Avoid the communication extremes of overdramatization and sugarcoating. Your team members are adults who can handle facts without embellishment. And remember that most people are turned off by what they perceive as unrealistic claims, goals, and promises. Things that seem *too good to be true*, usually are – and your employees know it. When it comes to your communications, be positive and upbeat. Tell it like you see it … just don't *oversell* it.

COMMUNICATION OBSTACLES

... to Check For and Avoid

- Technical language that is not commonly understood

- Ambiguous words that can be interpreted differently
  (a lot, sometimes, usually, most of the time)

- Opinions portrayed as facts

- Binary words *(always, never)*

- Distracting gestures and body language

- Assumptions

- Negativity

- Too much information ... too many key points

- Typos and poor grammar

- Using media that is inappropriate for the message
  (e.g., sending an email or text when face-to-face is more appropriate)

Take Away ... to Remember

Communication is the most important tool in your leadership toolbox. It determines how people perceive you and how they respond to you. Your success as a leader will be determined by the degree to which you follow the third commandment of leadership:

COMMUNICATE WITH CARE AND CONVICTION

CREATE THE INVOLVEMENT YOU SEEK

Not too long ago we were working with the leadership group of a large telecommunications company to help them install a new performance management system throughout their organization. In one of our many meetings, we asked the participants about the problems and challenges they were facing and the things they would like to see changed. Several of the leaders in the room expressed the same concern: a lack of employee involvement and participation. As one member of the group put it:

Many of our people are apathetic. They just do what they're told and nothing more. They're not committed or really involved in what we do.

We weren't surprised by that description – we had heard it many times before (and since). But the group *was* surprised by our response:

So, what are you doing about it?

One of the leaders in the room immediately suggested that we were talking to the wrong people ... that we should be talking to employees about this issue. We explained the error of her thinking with this fact: Team members typically fail to become involved for one of three reasons:

1. **They lack motivation** (i.e., there's no perceived benefit).
2. **They lack opportunities** to truly participate in meaningful ways.
3. **They lack the skills and confidence** needed to contribute.

All of those factors are things that leaders either directly control or have a strong ability to influence. They are within any leader's purview. They are within *your* purview. And that is why the fourth commandment of leadership is:

Create the Involvement You Seek.

Influencing Motivation

When individuals and teams are motivated, extraordinary things happen. Employees don't simply perform their jobs; they attack them – eager to make contributions. And the results are obvious: customers are delighted, the workplace is energized, innovations – large and small – happen with regularity, revenues are healthy, and the organization continually grows and develops.

So how can you motivate your team members to be more involved and engaged in their jobs? Well, the academic answer is you can't! Motivation is internal – it comes from deep within each of us. The only person who can truly motivate a person *is* the person. But, although you can't control motivation, you certainly can affect it. You can create conditions where employees want to be motivated and therefore motivate themselves. And here's one you can take to the bank: With few exceptions, all people want to achieve, contribute, and be a part of something special. Our inherent drive challenges us to achieve. Your task as a leader is to harness and nurture that drive … to feed it and help it to grow.

How do you do that? **By focusing on and adjusting consequences!** You have to increase the positive consequences that come (or at least *should* come) with greater involvement, and decrease the negative, frustrating ones that discourage involvement as well.

Talk to your people. Ask them about the pluses and minuses – the "upsides and downsides" they perceive are linked to greater involvement, commitment, and initiative. Solicit their input on what you can do to encourage even more contributions on their part. Then ACT on what you hear. And remember to thank them for their input. The simple act of responding to your questions is the start of increased participation.

Creating Opportunities ... Giving them a voice and a say

"If only my people would act more
like partners in this business."

Sound familiar? That's a fairly common management lament. And chances are you've thought or said it yourself at one time or another. If so, there is good news – here's a general rule of thumb that will serve you well throughout your leadership career:

If you want team members to act more like partners,
TREAT THEM MORE LIKE PARTNERS!

If that seems like no big revelation, you're right. It's just common sense. People tend to act according to how they're treated ... according to what they perceive they ARE. Expect team members to check their brains at the door when they come in, and that's precisely what many will do – they'll respond as mere "cogs in a wheel." But provide them with real opportunities to participate and be involved – give them more of "a voice and a say" in your daily operation – and they'll take more ownership of it. It truly IS that simple.

Giving employees **a voice** means fostering a workplace in which team members' ideas and concerns are solicited, welcomed, considered, and appreciated. It's about taking full advantage of the brainpower existing within your group. And it all starts with four small, yet unbelievably powerful, words – the same ones you want to hear from those to whom you report:

"What do YOU think?"

Giving employees **a say** means allowing team members to make work-related decisions whenever appropriate and practical. It's about delegating authority along with responsibility ... about taking participation to the next level (beyond just providing input) ... about communicating goals and parameters – and then uttering four more powerful words:

"YOU make the call."

More importantly, it's about understanding and accepting two facts of business life: 1) As a leader, you WILL always be responsible for ensuring that the best decisions are made, and 2) You WON'T always be the best person to make those decisions.

So, look for opportunities to give your team members more of a voice and a say in your operation. You'll end up with more ideas and better decisions. You'll help your people learn and grow. And, since people tend to support that which they influence and help to create, you'll likely experience greater employee commitment to the tasks at hand ... and to you.

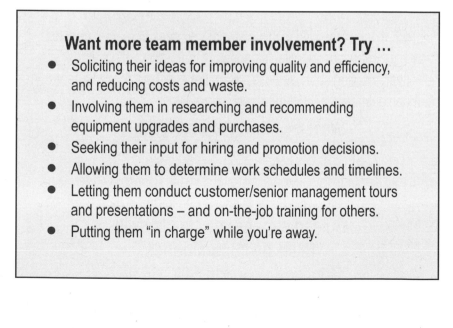

Want more team member involvement? Try ...

- Soliciting their ideas for improving quality and efficiency, and reducing costs and waste.
- Involving them in researching and recommending equipment upgrades and purchases.
- Seeking their input for hiring and promotion decisions.
- Allowing them to determine work schedules and timelines.
- Letting them conduct customer/senior management tours and presentations – and on-the-job training for others.
- Putting them "in charge" while you're away.

Building Skills and Confidence

To be sure, you must create opportunities for team members to have meaningful participation and become engaged in your mission and business activities. But your role as a leader doesn't stop there. You also need to provide guidance and support ... to help them build the skills and confidence necessary to seize those opportunities *successfully.*

For example ...

> If you want to push more decision-making down to the employee level, you need to teach those employees what's involved – what information they need to gather ... what things they need to weigh, consider, and evaluate before making a call.

> If you want team members to present their ideas and suggestions to you and members of senior management, you need to help them hone their data gathering and communication skills.

> If you want your people to lead meetings, provide them with resources that offer effective meeting management techniques.

So, take stock of the kind of involvement you seek from your people. Create as many opportunities as possible. Take some risks. And if you ever avoid expanding those possibilities because you feel your team members just can't handle them, ask yourself:

What am I doing to change that?

Opportunity builds experience.
Guided experience builds skills.
Skills build confidence.
Confidence builds SUCCESS.

Involvement "Turn-Offs" for Team Members

- No acknowledgment/response to their ideas and suggestions
- No *serious* consideration given to their input
- Being delegated responsibility without authority
- Failure to receive thanks and credit for ideas that are used
- Fear of reprisal for offering candid feedback
- Fear of being punished for unintentional mistakes
- Being micromanaged
- Superficial ("for show") rather than substantive participation opportunities
- Additional work and effort with no commensurate rewards

The fewer of these that exist in your organization, the more involvement you'll experience and enjoy!

Take Away ... to Remember

With few exceptions, employees want to participate in, and contribute to, your organization's important mission. If provided with meaningful opportunities – along with the requisite skills for success – they will engage. As a leader, you need to make that happen ... you need to follow the fourth leadership commandment:

CREATE THE INVOLVEMENT YOU SEEK

Do Right By Those Who Do Right

Some people call it "positive reinforcement," others, a "motivational strategy." Still others label it "common courtesy" – a sign of appreciation. But most folks refer to it as "RECOGNITION." And it's one of the biggest *un*kept secrets in business today!

Why an "*un*kept secret"? Well, there's certainly no shortage of research and expert opinion on the positive impacts of recognition in the workplace. Studies show that recognition fosters job satisfaction, builds self-esteem, and reinforces desired performance. It supports quality, strengthens trust and loyalty, and helps shape "magnetic" cultures that attract and keep the very best people. Yet, despite these (and a lot more) widely accepted and well-documented benefits, far too many recognition opportunities are being missed in far too many organizations, every day. And chances are, you're both a victim *of* – and contributor *to* – that reality.

Here's a short, two-question survey that you'll probably be able to answer without investing very much think time:

1. Ever feel unappreciated or underrecognized for the good work you do?
2. Ever miss opportunities to recognize your team members for the good work that they do?

If you're like most folks, your answers were "yes" and "yes." All of us occasionally feel taken for granted. We know how bad that feels. And when we fail to acknowledge the contributions of our people, we pass along that same lousy feeling. We do it not because we're bad people, but because we're human … and we sometimes lose sight of what's truly important. But we can change that. YOU can change that – by following the fifth commandment of leadership:

Do Right By Those Who Do Right.

How It *Should* Be

When team members do what you want them to do – when they meet your expectations or go above and beyond the call of duty – there ought to be something in it for them. And that something needs to be more than just "continued employment." But for more employees than you might think, the scenario goes like this: Do bad and you get "called on the carpet"; do well and you get *nothing* – except the chance to come back tomorrow and relive the scenario all over again. Certainly, there are many ways to inspire and motivate people, but **that's NOT one of them!**

Think of it this way: You want your people to meet your performance and behavior expectations, right? Obviously! And when they do, is your job easier and more satisfying? Sure! And of course, anyone who makes your job easier deserves your appreciation, right? Absolutely! Then why wouldn't you *show* your gratitude to those folks? NO REASON!

Of all the activities you engage in as a leader,
"catching people doing things right" –
and recognizing them for it –
needs to be one of your top priorities.

Whether it's a tangible reward (when appropriate), a special benefit, or just a sincere "thank you," the act of recognizing team members sends two messages: **good performance matters** and **your efforts and contributions are known and appreciated.** You don't have to be a psychologist to know that messages like those can positively affect employee motivation and satisfaction.

Fact:

Recognizing good performance gets you MORE of it

Why? Because whenever you recognize any behavior,

you also reinforce it. And, with few exceptions, …

REINFORCED BEHAVIOR IS REPEATED BEHAVIOR!

Knowing What to Look For

Make a list of "doing right" behaviors and achievements for your work group. Jot down everything you can think of. Add to the list periodically. Most importantly, keep an eye out for people who DO the things on your list and recognize them! Here is a handful of recognition opportunities to get your list started:

- Long-term positive performance – such as perfect attendance for six months or a year

- Exceeding expectations – like completing a project ahead of schedule

- Volunteering for a difficult assignment

- Helping others in the organization meet *their* goals

- Displaying contagious enthusiasm

- Submitting a cost-saving or time-saving idea

- Requesting/accepting additional responsibilities

- Going "above and beyond" for a customer or colleague

- Keeping a cool head under pressure

- Being a dependable team player who delivers quality work and causes you zero problems or headaches

DOING RIGHT BY THOSE WHO DO RIGHT CHECKLIST

Make sure the recognition you provide is ...

☐ TIMELY

Don't wait. Acknowledge the performance or contribution as soon as possible after it takes place. Praise tends to lose its effectiveness with the passing of time.

☐ SPECIFIC

Tell team members exactly what they did that was right and good. A mere "nice job" doesn't really say all that much. Being specific lets employees know exactly what behaviors to repeat in the future.

☐ SINCERE

Insincere praise is usually worse than no praise at all. Be honest and open. Tell team members what their positive performance means to you personally.

☐ INDIVIDUAL

Focus on individuals rather than groups. Fact is, not all team members contribute equally – and they know it.

☐ PERSONAL

Adjust the style and method of your recognition to each receiver. Some people like public praise ... others prefer private chats; some respond well to tangible tokens ... others would rather have some extra time off.

☐ PROPORTIONAL

Match the amount and intensity of your recognition to the value of the achievement. Going overboard for small contributions may lead people to question your motives.

Tips and Techniques

■ **Diversify!** Don't get in a rut by providing the same kind of recognition all the time – mix it up. Use a variety of verbal "well dones," written commendations, awards, perks, developmental opportunities, special assignments, etc. You'll make it more meaningful for your people and a lot more enjoyable for you!

■ Here's a question to ask new people who join your team: **"When you do good work and contribute to the team, how do you like to be recognized?"** You'll not only learn about what motivates people, but you'll also begin establishing an expectation that team members will do a good job! This great "double hit" technique really is effective.

■ You can increase the impact of your recognition by linking performance to "big picture" end states. Rather than just saying, "Wow, you really handled that well," try something like: "What you did really enhanced our relationship with a very important client. I'm convinced she will do business with us again soon. And you're a big reason for that."

■ **Check *your* facts!** Make sure people truly deserve praise *before* you give it. The only thing worse than insincere recognition is unearned recognition – especially when it's seen by others who know what's really going on!

■ **Establish "recognizing team members" as a performance expectation** for any leaders who report to you. Discuss it during staff meetings, coaching sessions, and performance reviews. Require your leaders to identify how they are contributing to a culture of appreciation. Remember that people tend to do what's EXpected when it's INspected!

■ Don't forget to acknowledge and thank "behind the scenes" people who contribute to your organization's success. For example, praise the accounts receivable clerk who enhanced your relationship with a slow-paying customer, or celebrate the positive comment you received from a vendor about your attentive receptionist.

Team members' perceptions are their realities.
Regardless of your good intentions and actions,
people who work with and for you are recognized
and appreciated only when they *feel* they are.
It's not enough to focus merely on what you *do;*
you also must be concerned with what they *think*
about what you do!

Take Away ... to Remember

When team members perform well – when they meet or exceed your expectations – when they live up to their responsibilities and contribute to the organization's mission, they deserve positive consequences in return. As the leader, it's up to you to give them what they have rightfully earned. It's up to you to remember and apply the fifth leadership commandment:

DO RIGHT BY THOSE WHO DO RIGHT

PROVIDE WHAT THEY NEED TO SUCCEED

Why does my leadership position exist?
What is my ultimate purpose?
Why am I here?

Those are three rather profound questions that most leaders spend little, if any, time pondering. If you're one of those who hasn't thought much about your role, here's some enlightenment …

Your leadership position exists for two primary purposes:

1. **To support and advance the organization's mission**
2. **To help employees reach their potential for success**

Clearly, those roles are inextricably linked. The more successful your team members are, the more fulfilled your organization's mission will be. Support your people and you automatically support your mission. And in doing that, nothing is more important than ensuring that employees *can* do well – that they're *allowed* to do well – by EQUIPPING them to do well!

For the most part, all team members want to be successful. But they require help … they need *things*. It's tough for people to do a good job – to do their best work – when they don't have the "tools" (resources) they need. That's something your team members may be facing more often than you think. And as a leader, you need to do *your* best to do something about it. You need to make sure your people's achievements are happening *because* of how they are equipped, not *in spite* of it. We all need to do that! So, pay close and special attention to the sixth commandment of leadership:

Provide What They Need to Succeed.

What They Need

The things your team members need in order to be as successful as possible typically fall within three categories. You need to provide …

_____ 1. INFORMATION _____

■ **Clear expectations.** Team members should know – in specific, behavioral terms – what they need to do to be successful in your eyes. Some "leaders" never take the time to clarify their performance expectations – rationalizing that lack of communication with statements such as: "It's on the job description" … "They've been here long enough – they should know by now" … "They'll figure it out just like I did." In effect, the position each of those managers has taken is: *I expect my people to do what it is I haven't told them.*

■ **Ongoing feedback.** Ask any group of people how often they receive detailed feedback on their performance at work and it's not unusual to hear: "Only at annual review time … or if I really screw up." That's truly unfortunate. And it's definitely unfair for those team members who are left in the dark. Common sense suggests that the more employees know how they stack up against your expectations, the easier it is for them to keep their performance on track. That's why providing specific, detailed feedback needs to be an ongoing process rather than a once-a-year "event."

■ **Task-specific data.** Employees must have all pertinent background information in order to perform tasks properly and carry out delegated responsibilities. This includes the whats, whys, and whens of things that must be done; any requirements that must be met and restrictions that must be followed; what latitude and discretion can be exercised; how success will be measured and evaluated; and who to turn to for guidance and assistance. Deliver this information and you help your people deliver "the goods."

2. RESOURCES
The 4 T's ...

■ **Time.** If you want people to perform at their best, you must ensure that they have adequate time to do so. Unrealistic timeframes and deadlines are obstacles to peak performance. They produce anger and frustration; they tempt people to cut corners and settle for "good enough."

Effective leaders not only provide time, they also respect it. If you want team members to believe that their work is important, you have to believe it, too. More importantly, you have to behave like you believe it! Don't expect people to drop whatever they're doing every time you want or need something. Instead, ask if they have a few minutes to chat. Better yet, ask for a time when they'll be available to meet with you.

■ **Tools.** Imagine this scenario: You're out in the middle of a field and your boss gives you an assignment to dig a trench. After explaining why the trench is necessary, he gives you the go-ahead to start digging. You inquire, "Where's the backhoe?" He responds, "It's in the shop." You then ask, "So how am I supposed to dig this trench?" He hands you a shovel and leaves. He returns two hours later and finds that you haven't made much progress. You're tired and frustrated ... and he's ticked off.

A far-fetched story? Maybe so. But it does make a simple and important point: Failing to provide team members with the "tools" they need is setting them up for failure. And that's just the opposite of what you should be doing. Obviously, very few people in the world actually dig trenches. But every job requires certain equipment, devices, software, and supplies. Your people are responsible for doing good work. You are responsible for making sure that's possible.

- **Training.** It's almost impossible to do a job well if you don't know how. That's why one of the most basic (and sometimes overlooked) success strategies is making sure that each team member has the knowledge and skills required to meet job expectations. Ask yourself this question:

    How sure am I that each employee has received
    proper training in all aspects of the job?

    Unless you're positive that the instruction provided has been adequate and appropriate, arrange for more. You probably have a variety of developmental resources at your disposal – such as manuals, classes, computer-based programs, and on-the-job training. So use them!

- **"Troops."** One of the many responsibilities of leadership is making sure there is adequate staffing to get the work done. Even though "doing more with less" has become – and likely will continue to be – the business mantra of this ever-tightening economy, you must be cautious and careful not to drive your people into the ground with more work than they can reasonably be expected to handle. To be sure, almost everyone these days must accept the requirement to work harder and smarter. But as they're doing that, you must do your best to arrange schedules and staff assignments so that "enough" team members are available for important tasks and projects.

Oftentimes, what team members *really* need
in order to be successful are a few
extra sets of hands to help carry the load.

3. SUPPORT

How to SUPPORT Your Team Members

Maintain an "Open Door." Encourage them to come to you with their problems and concerns. Listen and respond appropriately.

Be accessible and available. Unless you're on personal leave, make sure they can contact you for any needed clarification or guidance.

Allow reasonable schedule flexibility to accommodate their personal needs.

Think and plan before assigning work and implementing projects so you can minimize unnecessary changes and extra work.

Keep the environment respectful and "safe." Do not allow derogatory humor, destructive feedback, or the criticizing of input and ideas. Take immediate action to stop them if they occur.

Back their decisions and act on their recommendations whenever possible and appropriate.

Run interference. Be a "go-between" to help team members get any required senior management approvals and interdepartmental cooperation.

Minimize obstacles. Identify any organizational factors (including your behaviors) that inhibit team member success. Eliminate or minimize those obstacles as best you can.

Be familiar with employee assistance programs available within your organization. Recommend them to team members in need.

Most employees can be much more successful
than they are. And when it comes to that,
as a leader, you're either part of the
solution ... or you're part of the problem.

How to Discover What Else Team Members Need for Success

Ask them!

Take Away ... to Remember

Like you, team members want to do well and make positive contributions
to the organization. But also like you, they need help to do that ... they
need information, resources, and support. And they need those things
from YOU. As a leader, your success comes from your people's success.
So, one of the very best things you can do for them *and yourself* is
practice leadership commandment number six:

PROVIDE WHAT THEY NEED TO SUCCEED

CONFRONT CHALLENGES WITH COURAGE

Another of the many characteristics shared by true leaders is having the courage to make tough decisions and take difficult actions. That's why "leadership" and "courage" are often viewed as synonymous concepts.

The dictionary definition of *courage* is "the state or quality of mind and spirit that enables one to face danger or fear with confidence and resolution; bravery; valor." But what does all that mean in the business world? What does it look like? How can it be measured and quantified?

Perhaps the best way to understand courage is to define its opposite state. Many would suggest the antithesis of courage is "cowardliness" ... avoiding or succumbing to pressure, difficulty, and danger. Others would say "fear" ... being afraid to do the right thing when the going gets tough. And there are those who would offer "conformity" ... letting things continue the way they are because of the high price associated with changing them. ALL of those definitions are valid and appropriate.

As a leader, you need courage to do what is expected of you ... to do what you're *there* to do. You will encounter coworkers who believe your actions are wrong – even when you're thoroughly convinced that you're right. There will be situations that tempt you to take an easier and less resistant path. And there will be people who – either unintentionally or purposefully – create obstacles that will challenge your tenacity and resolve.

Even the very best leaders must occasionally pass the courage test. The true measure of your leadership effectiveness is the ability to look in the mirror and know that you had the strength and courage to do what, deep down inside, you knew was the right thing to do. And it's that very fact that leads to the seventh leadership commandment:

Confront Challenges with Courage.

Tough Calls

A good team member who has earned special consideration asks for time off. Granting her request would leave you overly short-staffed. You want to say "yes" – but doing so will jeopardize the work that needs to be done for an important client.

A critical project that impacts several departments has fallen behind schedule. The only way to get back on track is to require additional weekend overtime from an already overworked and very tired team.

A long-tenured and well-liked employee has put in for a promotion. The rest of the team assumes he'll get the job – but you know he's not really qualified to do what's needed to meet current and future needs.

Three different situations … three tough calls to make … one common requirement: courage on your part to do what you know must be done!

Scenarios like those described above (and many, many more) occur every day in all types of industries and business organizations. Chances are you've actually faced similar situations yourself, and you know, first-hand, how difficult they are to deal with. Yes, they are challenging – but they are part of your leadership responsibilities … they do "come with the territory." And regardless of how many stress-free days you wish to experience – or how much you may want to be liked by the people with whom you work – one simple fact always remains …

> You can't be a true leader by following the crowd,
> trying to please people, or taking the easy way out.
> Those are "luxuries" you no longer enjoy.

Doing what's right isn't always easy – but it is always right. Make the tough calls!

Performance Issues

By far, some of the most intense and gut-wrenching challenges leaders ever face fall in the category labeled with these three dreaded words:

Employee Performance Problems.

Many agree that it's the absolute worst part of their jobs. Having to look someone in the eye and tell them they're "not cutting it" is tough. And because it's so unpleasant, you may be tempted to "look the other way" until either the problem goes away on its own (which rarely to never happens), or it becomes so serious and impacting that you have no choice but to act – often in anger. Don't succumb to that temptation! It's one of the most unfair things you could do to any team member.

As a leader, your job is to help, guide, and motivate employees to be as successful as they can possibly be. And knowing that someone has a performance problem – but saying or doing nothing about it – is NOT the way you meet that responsibility. Fact is, there just are no valid excuses for inaction on your part – other than you lack the courage to do what needs to be done.

Addressing and resolving employee performance problems is your duty. It's something you owe to all team members – not just the few with issues, but also the majority of hard-working contributors who count on you to ensure that everyone pulls their weight. So, forget the excuses. Don't wait. Deal with performance discrepancies as soon as you become aware of them. Work through any fear, anxiety, or discomfort you may have. Fact is, the earlier you address issues, the less chance there is that you'll end up facing the toughest task of all: letting the person go.

Interpersonal Conflicts

Wherever there are people working together, there *will* be tension and strife. Count on it. Expect it. Sooner or later, it's going to happen – a conflict will surface between two or more of your team members, and it won't be pleasant. Perhaps you'll see it in their behaviors; maybe someone else on the team will clue you in. How you find out about it doesn't matter. What *does* matter is what you do about it. Once again, you're faced with a difficult situation requiring courage on your part.

When two employees are at odds with each other, the tension and stress of conflict spill over onto other members of the team as well. Their co-workers don't want to "take sides" or "walk on eggshells," and they must deal with – and often compensate for – the counterproductive behaviors that typically result from other people's souring relationships. All that makes it difficult for them to do *their* very best work – and, as a leader, that makes dealing with the conflict YOUR BUSINESS!

So, don't allow interpersonal conflicts between team members to fester. Keep your eyes and ears open for potential problems and get involved. Meet with the "combatants" to explain your concerns and confirm that a problem exists. Describe how others are impacted and clarify your expectation that the parties will work together to resolve the issue. Work with them to develop action plans, and then follow up to make sure progress is being made.

Conflicts are workplace obstacles. Don't let them get in the way of your team's success. Dealing with them may not be pleasant. But having to repair the damage they can cause will be even worse.

Courage is ...

✓ Following your conscience instead of "following the crowd."

✓ Taking action against hurtful or disrespectful behaviors.

✓ Sacrificing personal gain for the benefit of others.

✓ Speaking your mind even though others don't agree.

✓ Taking complete responsibility for your actions ... and your mistakes.

✓ Following the rules – and insisting that others do the same.

✓ Hiring and promoting people who are faster, smarter, and more talented than you are.

✓ Challenging the status quo in search of better ways.

✓ Facing setbacks and disappointments head-on – without losing your drive and spirit or adopting a victim mentality.

✓ Telling others what they *need* to hear rather than what they *want* to hear.

✓ Doing what you know is right – regardless of the risks and potential consequences.

Do these traits and characteristics describe YOU?

Make us choose the harder right
instead of the easier wrong,
and never to be content with half truth
when whole can be won.
Endow us with courage that is born
of loyalty to all that is noble and worthy,
that scorns to compromise with vice
and injustice and knows no fear
when truth and right are in jeopardy.

Excerpt from Cadet Prayer repeated during
chapel services at the U.S. Military Academy

Take Away ... to Remember

Leadership is not for the faint of heart. Along with your title comes many awesome responsibilities – and an equal number of situations that can and will test your mettle. And one thing is for sure: Your effectiveness as a leader will be determined by how well you pass those tests ... by how well you practice the seventh commandment of leadership:

CONFRONT CHALLENGES WITH COURAGE

LET DIFFERENCES BECOME YOUR DIRECTION

Ever find yourself thinking that people who are "different" from you (different ethnicity, age, gender, way of speaking, way of thinking, way of approaching tasks and solving problems, etc.) are weird, wrong, problematic (or something worse)? Of course! We all occasionally fall into that trap. And whenever *you* do, you'd be wise to stop, tap yourself on the back of the head, and re-evaluate (i.e., change) your viewpoint. That's bogus thinking ... and there's no place for it within the ranks of leadership.

Here's the reality: Each of us is unique ... no two people are exactly the same. So, if being different equated to being wrong, EVERYONE WOULD BE WRONG – including YOU! That would definitely be bad. But you know what would be worse? If everyone were exactly alike! In that case, we'd all look, sound, and act the same. We'd only need one type of food, one way of thinking, one sport, one channel on our televisions, one kind of music, one make of car, one style of clothes, one political party – simply one of everything.

With everyone the same, we wouldn't have creative "oddballs" inventing new technologies and creature comforts to improve our lives; we wouldn't have "foreigners" buying our products and services; we wouldn't have the blending of cultures and ideas that afford us new and enriching experiences. And you wouldn't have individual employees bringing the varied skills, ideas, and strengths you rely on for your organization's (and your) ongoing success.

You see, diversity in the workplace (in all its forms) is not something to be feared or squelched – it's an advantage to be nurtured and encouraged. And that's the precise reason why leadership commandment number eight is ...

Let Differences Become Your Direction.

The Real Enemy

It's a question we've asked business leaders hundreds of times over the past several years:

What's the biggest threat your organization faces?

By far, the most consistent response we've received:

Competition!

And while there certainly is validity to that answer, there's an even greater threat that you, as a leader, must address – and it does not come from the outside. It's internal. And it goes by many names such as "Business as Usual," "The Way We Do Things," and "Same Ol' Same Ol'." Its most common moniker: THE STATUS QUO. It's implication – sameness.

To be sure, the status quo provides familiarity, comfort, and a sense of stability. But, far too often, those feel-good factors lead to complacency and coasting. We focus on repetition rather than improvement … on activities rather than advances … on today rather than tomorrow. And we eventually find ourselves in an ironic "catch 22" – the behaviors and approaches that brought us initial success are the very same ones that are now preventing us from enjoying further success. As the saying goes,

> If you keep on doing what you've always done,
> you'll keep on getting what you've always got.

And that's just not good enough to survive and prosper in today's highly competitive, rapidly changing business environment.

Think about it. Pretty much ALL of the successes you now enjoy resulted from being different – in some way – than you were before. So common sense dictates that future successes can come only by being different than you are now. The "good old days" are old … and gone.

Fact:

*Workforces and the teams that comprise them
are more diverse now than ever before.
That's not a problem – it's an advantage!*

Dealing with the Reality of Differences
Questions to Answer:

What can we do to better understand and appeal to
a changing marketplace and customer base?

How can we take full advantage of the diverse backgrounds and
experiences of our changing workforce demographics?

How can advances in technology help us be more
efficient and effective?

How can we work smarter in order to "do more with less"?

How can we separate ourselves from – and outperform –
our business competitors?

What can we do to be more "green" in protecting
our resources … and our planet?

What behaviors must everyone adopt in order to encourage
more creativity and innovation?

How is our work, our industry, and our economy changing –
and what are we doing in response to those changes?

7 Ways to Make Differences Your Direction

1. Hire and Promote People Who Are "Different"

Staff your organization – and your team – with people who bring unique backgrounds, experiences, ideas, skills, and abilities to relate to a diverse customer population. And, by all means, avoid any temptations to search for and bring on your personal clones. You really don't need more people thinking exactly like you or doing exactly what you do. You're already here!

2. Encourage "Out of the Box" Problem Solving

Teach, use, and reinforce creative thinking and problem-solving techniques like brainstorming. Get in the habit of using phrases like: "What if we ..." and "Here's a crazy idea ..." – and avoid verbiage such as "That will never work." Don't be quick to evaluate or discount ideas and suggestions – allow them to be expressed, considered, tweaked, and built upon. And never "run" with the first idea you have or hear unless you're absolutely positive that it's a winner.

3. Keep the Environment "Safe"

Make sure that all team members feel comfortable sharing ideas without fear of criticism or being laughed at. Make it clear that behaviors which inhibit or discourage the free-flow of creative ideas are unacceptable. And set the expectation that everyone will participate. With few exceptions, each team member has something to contribute ... something that can benefit the group's and the organization's mission.

When ideas are left unspoken, everyone loses.

4. Support Intelligent Risk Taking

Let everyone on your team know that taking risks in trying new things is not only okay, it's encouraged – as long as it's done intelligently. That means doing appropriate research, considering alternatives, and thinking things through before taking action. It means having a belief, an educated hunch, a reason for doing something – rather than merely shooting in the dark. And, for you the leader, it means accepting that with risk comes failure as well as success.

5. Provide Freedom with Fences

Set the parameters (timetables, budgets, goals, etc.) for projects and assignments, but allow team members discretion on *how* they tackle those tasks. Of course, proper procedures – especially those that relate to safety and ethics – must be followed. That's a given. But what need not be a given is the way people operate within established guidelines.

> Avoid "there's only one way to do this" mindsets and you'll open the door for new and innovative approaches.

6. Cherish the Challengers

Think team members who periodically question procedures and challenge the way things get done are a disruptive pain? If so, you might want to do a little rethinking. Those folks just may be some of your most valuable business assets. Why? Because, typically, they're the ones who refuse to blindly accept the status quo … they're the ones who willingly share their thoughts, beliefs, and concerns … they're the ones who pave the roads to improvement and success. So, the next time someone on your team questions an approach or strategy, don't roll your eyes – extend your hand, say thank you, and ask the person for his or her thoughts on what types of productive changes might be made.

7. Do a "Uniqueness Inventory"

Write down the names of all of your team members. Next to each name, list what's unique and special about the person that could be beneficial to the team and your organization. Include things like skills, experiences, languages spoken, creativity, analytical prowess, ability to perform under pressure, etc. Ask each employee to identify their own personal strengths and add those characteristics to your list. Then review your total list. Chances are you'll be surprised (and quite pleased) with all the "differences" at your disposal that can help you meet today's and tomorrow's business needs. Finally, strategize ways to tackle your biggest challenge of all: taking full advantage of what you have!

There's only one thing you can accurately
predict about the future:
IT WILL BE DIFFERENT

Take Away ... to Remember

Leadership is not about keeping people and organizations where they are. Rather, it's about maximizing their potential ... taking them where they need to go in order to be winners. You've been blessed with more diversity ... more choices ... more options ... more "tools" than have existed in any other time in history. Tomorrow's success is there for the taking if you follow the eighth commandment of leadership and

LET DIFFERENCES BECOME YOUR DIRECTION

STRIVE TO SERVE OTHERS

Serving Your Team

How do you view the members of your team? Do you see them as the people who work for you? Most leaders do. Obviously, employees report to you, they take direction from you, they are accountable to you. You are "the boss" – and maybe you worked your way up from an entry (or at least *lower*) level position. Now it's your turn to call the shots – and you have a "staff" to do what you need and want done. Your people are there to serve customers ... and they're there to serve you, right? Sure! But, while it's technically accurate, that type of thinking is also limiting when it comes to leadership effectiveness. And a little mindset adjustment would serve you well. There is a much better – and broader – perspective to adopt:

Instead of just seeing your team as people who work for you, try thinking of them – and referring to them – also as the people YOU WORK FOR!

Go ahead ... try it now. Can you feel the difference? Without question, it's a more collaborative, more service-focused, more "working together to accomplish common goals" viewpoint. And besides, it's true. You DO work for your team! They are the individuals your time and efforts are geared toward. They are the people you guide ... the people you lead. They depend on you to help them be successful. And you owe it to them to be the very best leader you can be. In that sense, you are here to help and serve them. And, **you are accountable to them.**

THE LEADERSHIP PARADOX

The people who work for you also are the people for whom you work!

You Serve Others When You ...

 Make providing exceptional customer service a performance requirement for everyone on your team.

✓ Demonstrate respect and empathy for every individual.

✓ Tell people what they *need* to hear rather than *want* to hear.

✓ Hold team members accountable for doing quality work.

 Contribute to others' success and well-being.

 Make sure that everyone on the team does his or her share.

✓ Keep everyone focused on the organization's mission.

✓ Maintain a positive, productive, and safe working environment.

✓ Set the example and tone for everyone to follow.

 Provide resources and information, and remove obstacles.

✓ Do what's right ... what needs to be done – regardless of how difficult it may be.

✓ Hire and promote people of quality.

✓ Help team members learn, develop, grow, and achieve their personal goals.

✓ Know the way and show the way.

✓ Commit to being the very best leader you can be.

✓ **Embrace and practice THE 10 COMMANDMENTS OF LEADERSHIP.**

The "Sounds" of Service

The **10** important sounds:
I apologize for the mistake. Let me make it right.

The **9** important sounds:
How can I make this job easier for you?

The **8** important sounds:
I'm not sure, but I will find out.

The **7** important sounds:
How can we do better next time?

The **6** important sounds:
What can I do to help?

The **5** important sounds:
Tell me what you need.

The **4** important sounds:
I'm here for you.

The **3** important sounds:
I'll handle that.

The **2** important sounds:
Thank you.

The **1** important sound:
Yes.

Do I SERVE Others?

A Self-Reflection Assessment

Do I ...

Seize opportunities to help others be more successful?

Enrich the experiences, careers, and lives of those with whom I interact?

Resist the temptation to think and act in "me first" ways?

Volunteer my time and efforts for the betterment of others?

Extend a "helping hand" to those in need?

It is the act of serving others that makes leadership a noble and rewarding professional calling.

_____

Take Away ... to Remember

With leadership comes a great deal of power and authority – the ability to direct, control, and decide. What separates true leaders from those who are "leaders" by title only is how they *use* that power and authority. Each of us must choose whether we will use our influence to serve ourselves – or those with and for whom we work. YOU must choose. Let the ninth commandment of leadership guide your choice ...

STRIVE TO SERVE OTHERS

Go Forth
and Prosper

This final chapter – and last leadership commandment – addresses one of the most important and significant lessons we've gleaned over the years – one that encapsulates the content of this book and the messages within it:

Effective leaders promote and protect prosperity.

Every great leader we have encountered has displayed a keen, perhaps inherent, awareness that true prosperity is a combination of achieving short-term financial gain *and* positioning their organizations for sustained, long-term success – and that working to make *both* of those end states workplace realities is a paramount responsibility of leadership.

Exceptional leaders believe that and they *behave* it. They move people in a forward direction with emphasis on progress and improvement. They encourage magnificence rather than settling for mediocrity. They focus on "means" (doing right) as well as "ends" (doing well). And they work on today's tasks with an eye on tomorrow's possibilities.

> Ultimately, what separates truly effective leaders from the "also leds" is their willing acceptance of the role of *Winner Maker.*

For them, job one is MAKING EVERYONE A WINNER – and included in that "everyone" is the organization, its management, its customers, its team members, and its stakeholders. Yes, great leaders accept that role. They cherish and honor that role. And so must you!

So, emulate the best of the best. If you do, you'll be practicing the tenth commandment of leadership:

Go Forth and Prosper.

It's About *Making More*

Some leaders believe that in order to achieve prosperity, they need to make more. And they're absolutely right! They *do* need to make more. YOU need to make more!

But that "more" cannot just be "more" salary or "more" perks. Sure, those benefits would be nice – and we certainly wouldn't turn them down if offered. However, truly effective leaders clearly understand that personal gain cannot be a singular objective. They understand that their organizations and their teams and they themselves prosper when they focus on ensuring that …

> *More* customers receive superior service;
>
> *More* goals are set and achieved;
>
> *More* skills are developed and honed by team members;
>
> *More* opportunities for growth are created;
>
> *More* recognition for positive contribution is given;
>
> *More* obstacles to performance are minimized or eliminated;
>
> *More* respect is demonstrated;
>
> *More* communication and better listening take place;
>
> *More* quality products and services are delivered;
>
> *More* cooperation and collaboration are evident;
>
> *More* information is shared;
>
> *More* successes are celebrated;
>
> *More* responsibility is assumed;
>
> *More* commitment and satisfaction are realized.

Effective leaders focus on these multiplier outcomes … and on, you guessed it, much *more*. Commit to following their lead.

Building upon Success

There's an old saying that's as true and relevant today as when it was first uttered:

Nothing succeeds like success!

Achievements, contributions, and positive outcomes make people feel good and important. They're motivating and uplifting. And when they are acknowledged and celebrated, their impacts often increase exponentially.

Winning fosters winning mindsets which, in turn, drive winning behaviors. Remember that natural phenomenon and use it to *everyone's* advantage.

Without question, successes should be sources of pride and enjoyment. But equally important, they are achievements to build upon. How do you do that? By studying, analyzing, and dissecting them. By identifying the activities and behaviors that made them successful – and applying that knowledge to future endeavors.

To succeed is to prosper. And **prosperity is a great path to additional prosperity.** So celebrate your team's successes. Recognize and reward them. Then, learn from them. Find out what's working well and do more of it.

Focusing on the Future

Effective leaders are future-oriented. They think about, focus on, and strategize for what is to come rather than what has been. They understand that *yesterday* is gone – and that *today* is on its way out. For them, the past serves but one purpose: to learn from in order to lead forward and shape a better *tomorrow*. And that is a mindset that you need to adopt as well.

Does that mean you should gloss over or ignore the issues of today? Of course not! Today is reality and you have to deal with it. But as you do, you must consider the implications and long-term impacts of your actions. The decisions you make, the plans you formulate, the people you hire, and the precedents you establish all should be done according to today's priorities – but with tomorrow's successes in mind.

The present does not exist in a vacuum –
it is directly linked to the future.
Each today is a building block of tomorrow.

Future-Oriented Questions to Answer
The Vision
*What level of success do I want for my organization
and my team ... in the next few years?*

The Action
*What can/will I do to begin to make that success
a reality ... in the next few weeks?*

Building a Lasting Legacy

For most folks, the word "legacy" conjures up mental images of historical people – "bigger than life," powerful, influential, and sometimes "saintly" individuals who have left indelible marks on the world around them. And in many cases, those people are no longer with us – living only in our memories. But while those images are accurate and valid, they represent only the tip of the legacy iceberg.

By its most basic definition, a legacy is how a person impacts others ... how he or she is thought of and remembered ... how conditions and circumstances are different (and hopefully better) because of his or her actions and influence. Anyone who interacts with and touches other people is creating a legacy of some kind. As a leader, you are building yours, right now; you're adding to it with each action you take or don't take ... each behavior you demonstrate or fail to display ... each thing you say or don't say.

So, think on this for a moment: If you resigned or retired tomorrow, what do you suppose your team members and colleagues would say about you? Would you be remembered? If so, how – and for what? Would people declare that you left them, and your organization, better than you found them? Would they want to be like you? Would they say "good leader" – or "good riddance"?

Okay, so you're not planning a major career change any time soon. You plan to be around for a while. GREAT! That means there's time to think about how you *want* to be remembered – and opportunities to mold those memories. Be the best leader you can be, and your legacy will be positive and lasting.

Preparing Others to Lead

Leadership effectiveness can be measured in many ways – using many different standards and criteria. Certainly, each organization has needs and requirements that its leaders must meet in order to ensure the ongoing viability and prosperity of the enterprise. Some of those needs are unique and proprietary; some are common and universal. And of those which are universal, one of the most critical of all is the need for MORE LEADERS.

Preparing and equipping team members to assume leadership roles is one of your key responsibilities. Arguably, it's the most important function you perform. And it's the very best way to multiply the impact you make and enhance the legacy you create.

Take Away ... to Remember

The primary responsibility of those in leadership positions is to help their organizations, and the people who comprise them, be more successful. You are the guide ... the pathfinder ... the point-person on a journey to greater possibilities and achievement. Your job is to take those you lead – and those you serve – to heights they likely would have great difficulty reaching by themselves. That is why you are here; that is why you are so critically important.

This tenth and final leadership commandment is more than a guideline – it's also an invitation ... a rallying cry ... a behavioral message for every-one on your team that says:

Follow my lead and together we all will
GO FORTH and PROSPER

Summary

The 10 Commandments of Leadership

1. Make What Matters Really Matter
Hold yourself and others accountable for bringing your mission to life.

2. Practice What You Preach
Be a role model for honesty, integrity, and walking the talk.

3. Communicate with Care and Conviction
*Share what you know, be considerate and confident,
and listen respectfully.*

4. Create the Involvement You Seek
Provide team members with meaningful opportunities to participate.

5. Do Right By Those Who Do Right
*Acknowledge and thank team members who meet or
exceed your expectations.*

6. Provide What They Need to Succeed
*Make sure team members have the tools, training, and
support necessary to do their best work.*

7. Confront Challenges with Courage
*Face difficult situations directly. Make the tough calls.
Do what you know needs to be done.*

8. Let Differences Become Your Direction
*Appreciate the uniqueness of all of your team members.
Use it to move you beyond the status quo.*

9. Strive to Serve Others
Use your knowledge and skills for the betterment of all "customers."

10. Go Forth and Prosper
*Build a lasting legacy. Accept that your ultimate purpose
is to help everyone become successful.*

CLOSING
THOUGHTS

As we stated in the introduction, experience is a wonderful teacher. It certainly has taught us well. And the great leaders we've had the good fortune to work with throughout our careers have taught us well. They have given us untold numbers of invaluable gifts by sharing *their* experiences about business – and about people. And in an effort to "pay it forward," we've compiled a collection of many of the lessons we've learned over the years – and passed them along to you in what we have labeled THE 10 COMMANDMENTS OF LEADERSHIP. But now you must decide what you will do with this information.

As written, the principles and guidelines presented in this book are just words … only good ideas. **You have to put them into ACTION in order for their value and benefits to be truly realized.** Perhaps our good friend and noted author, BJ Gallagher, said it best with her quote:

Success is the power of positive DOING.

To be sure, effective leadership requires more than noble principles and good intentions. You also need good practices. And those practices need to occur in a consistent and predictable fashion. Simply put, to be an effective leader, you must do the things that effective leaders DO!

Consider the exceptional leaders you have known about or experienced in the past. Reflect on the positive impact they've had on others … the positive impact they've had on *your* life and career. You now have that same opportunity to make a difference for the people you manage.

This is *your* time to "pay it forward."

As is true for all of us, things changed the moment you accepted your LEADERSHIP position. "The bar" was raised. Requirements went up, responsibilities went up, and expectations went up as well. You're now held to a higher standard – which is exactly as it should be. And that's not all. Along with your new title also came new functions, new tasks, and a new definition of – and pathway to – "success."

Now, you accomplish things through others. Now, the way you make a difference is by helping *your people* make a difference ... helping *them* be successful. Now, you must be as proficient in the business of leadership as you are in the business of your business. And your guide for achieving that success is THE 10 COMMANDMENTS OF LEADERSHIP.

So, keep this book handy. Reread it periodically and refer to it often.

Commit to following these simple and time-tested principles and you will be the effective and respected leader that all of your team members hope for and deserve.

The Authors

ERIC HARVEY, president and founder of WalkTheTalk.com, is a leading expert on Leadership, Ethics, and Values-Based Practices. He is a renowned business consultant and author of over 30 highly acclaimed books – including the best-selling *WALK the TALK, Ethics4Everyone,* and *The Leadership Secrets of Santa Claus*®. Eric and his team of professionals have helped thousands of individuals and organizations turn their values into value-added results.

STEVE VENTURA is a best-selling author, book producer, and award-winning training program designer. His work reflects over 30 years of management and human resource development experience – as both a practitioner and a business consultant. His prior books include *Start Right ... Stay Right, Walk Awhile in My Shoes, LEAD RIGHT, Five Star Teamwork, Conflict Happens, SERVE RIGHT,* and *Leadership Lessons*.

THE **10** COMMANDMENTS OF LEADERSHIP is Eric and Steve's sixth writing collaboration.

ABOUT WALKTHETALK.COM

For over 30 years, WalkTheTalk.com has been dedicated to one simple goal...one single mission: *To provide you and your organization with high-impact resources for your personal and professional success.*

Walk The Talk resources are designed to:

- Develop your skills and confidence
- Inspire your team
- Create customer enthusiasm
- Build leadership skills
- Stretch your mind
- Handle tough "people problems"
- Develop a culture of respect and responsibility
- And, most importantly, help you achieve your personal and professional goals.

Contact the Walk The Talk team at
1.888.822.9255
or visit us at *www.walkthetalk.com*

Resources for Personal and Professional Success

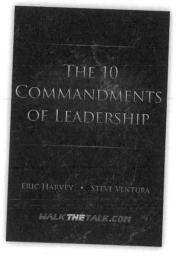

Take yourself and your leadership team
to the next level of EFFECTIVENESS with

THE 10 COMMANDMENTS OF LEADERSHIP
PERSONAL AND PROFESSIONAL SUCCESS KIT

Only $29.95

CONTAINS THE FOLLOWING RESOURCES:

■ **A copy of *The 10 Commandments of Leadership* book**

■ **A DVD containing:**
  - A 3-minute movie* that summarizes and reinforces the important 10 Commandments of Leadership principles

    Great meeting starter and training supplement!

  - Individual learning exercises and action planner to enhance your personal performance and build your leadership legacy

    Effective self-development tools – just for you!

  - Group discussion questions and learning exercises that encourage your leadership team to follow and apply *The 10 Commandments of Leadership* principles and strategies

    Perfect for leadership meetings and developmental activities!

To learn more, visit

WALKTHETALK.COM

*or to view the movie, visit **www.the10commandmentsofleadership.com**

Visit

WALKTHETALK.COM

Resources for Personal and Professional Success

to learn more about our:

Leadership & Personal Development Center

- Develop leadership skills
- Motivate your team
- Achieve business results

Free Newsletters

- Daily Inspiration
- The Power of Inspiration
- The Leadership Solution
- New Products and Special Offers

Motivational Gift Books

- Inspire your team
- Create customer enthusiasm
- Reinforce core values

The Greenhouse Bookstore

- Save time
- Save money
- Save the planet

**Contact the Walk The Talk team at 1.888.822.9255
or visit us at www.walkthetalk.com.**

Resources for Personal and Professional Success